CHAMP CARS

BY
JANE MERSKY LEDER

EDITED BY
DR. HOWARD SCHROEDER
Professor in Reading and Language Arts
Dept. of Elementary Education
Mankato State University

CREATED, DESIGNED, & PRODUCED BY

BAKER STREET PRODUCTIONS

CRESTWOOD HOUSE
Mankato, Minnesota

LIBRARY OF CONGRESS CATALOGING IN PUBLICATION DATA

Leder, Jane Mersky.
  Champ cars.

  (Technology)
  SUMMARY: A brief history of racing cars is followed by detailed descriptions of where and how these cars are built and tested. Includes a brief history of the Indy 500.
  1. Automobiles, Racing--Juvenile literature. (1. Automobiles, Racing. 2. Automobile racing.) I. Schroeder, Howard. II. Baker Street Productions. III. Title.
TL236.L43   1983   796.7'2   83-7877
ISBN 0-89686-238-0

International Standard Book Numbers:	**Library of Congress Catalog Card Number:**
Library Binding 0-89686-238-0	83-7877

PHOTO CREDITS

Alan Leder: Cover, 26, 27, 28, 29, 31, 33, 34, 35, 36, 39, 41
Dave Dwiggins: 4-5
Steve Snoddy: 7
Indianapolis Motor Speedway: 9, 10, 11, 13, 15, 18, 19, 20, 21, 23
Jim Haines: 25
Ron McQueeney: 43, 44

CRESTWOOD HOUSE
Hwy. 66 South, Box 3427
Mankato, MN 56002-3427

TABLE OF CONTENTS

ACKNOWLEDGMENT

A warm thank you to all the people at Patrick Racing Team. Without their help and cooperation, this book wouldn't have been possible.

INTRODUCTION

With thirteen laps remaining in a recent Indy 500, Gordon Johncock was leading the race by twelve seconds. A twelve-second lead with thirteen laps to go is big for most race car drivers. But this time it wasn't for Johncock. His left rear tire was overheating, pushing the front end of his Wildcat toward the wall on the outside turns.

"I was running as hard as I could go," he said after the race. "I was looking in my mirror and could see Rick Mears coming."

In 1982, the closest Indy 500 finish in history was won by Gordon Johncock by .16 of a second.

With four laps to go, Mears had pulled within three seconds of Johncock. With two laps left, John-cock's lead was 0.8 of a second. All 400,000 specta-tors were on their feet.

On the final lap Mears chased Johncock down the straightaway toward the checkered flag. Mears swung out in a final try to move ahead. But John-cock crossed the finish line slightly more than a car length ahead. He won by 0.16 of a second. It was the closest finish in the sixty-six-year history of the Indy 500.

Exciting finishes, sleek cars, and finely-tuned

engines that reach speeds of over two hundred mph — that's what brings race car fans back to the tracks every year. Nothing compares, say these fans, to the thrill of championship auto racing.

DIFFERENT KINDS OF RACE CARS

Race cars come in many shapes and sizes. The stock car, for example, looks just like an average family car. Its engine is "souped up" to make it go faster, and it has extra safety features. The sprint car is a faster, sleeker car. It has a front engine, wheels that are in the open, and a roll cage for safety. The Formula car, also called the Super V or Mini-Indy, looks like a miniature version of the championship car that races at the Indy 500. Unlike the championship car, however, it has a Volkswagon engine and can't go as fast. Formula One race cars also look a lot like championship cars but they only race on road courses. They never race on oval tracks. The Formula One race circuit is called the Grand Prix.

No race car gets as much attention as the championship (champ) car. It is in a class by itself. The champ car is considered by many people to be the most advanced and exciting race car. The world's best known race car drivers, like A. J. Foyt, Bobby and Al Unser, Mario Andretti, Johnny Rutherford, and Tom Sneva race champ cars. Every rookie, or beginning driver, dreams of someday racing a championship car.

THE CHAMPIONSHIP CAR RACE CIRCUIT

The championship car racing season starts at the end of March each year and ends on the first of

Cars come around the turn at the Indy 500.

November. Most champ car teams run in ten to twelve races during that time. There are races in Phoenix, Arizona; Atlanta, Georgia; Milwaukee, Wisconsin; and Cleveland, Ohio. The most popular, and most spectacular, race is held on the Sunday before Memorial Day in Indianapolis, Indiana. It's called the Indy 500. After time trials, the thirty-three fastest champ cars race five hundred miles in the hopes of winning the Superbowl of racing. It took a recent winner of the Indy 500, Gordon Johncock, just over three hours to complete the race. He earned the biggest share of the $1,600,000 in prize money.

HISTORY OF THE INDY 500 THE GREATEST SPECTACLE IN RACING

The first Indy 500 was held at the Indiana Motor Speedway in 1911. When the race track was designed in 1908, there wasn't a race track or test course anywhere in the world like it. The idea of a two and a half mile track in the shape of an oval, that could be seen from one big grandstand area, was brand new. The enclosed two and a half mile track was the first of its kind in the world.

Ray Harroun won the first Indy 500 in 1911. He drove a single-seater car named "Wasp." Mr. Har-

This 1909 photo shows the original asphalt and stone track.

roun won with an average speed of 74.59 mph.

The original track surface was a mixture of asphalt and crushed stone. But that mixture proved to be very dangerous. The first race turned into a blood bath. There were several crashes caused by punctured tires, flying stones, and poor traction. The whole Indy 500 idea almost stopped right there.

In fact, there were only two choices. Either give up the track or hard-pave it. Luckily for champ car racing, the owner of the speedway decided to hard-pave the track. Over three million, ten-pound bricks were laid in sixty-three days.

9

There are usually one hundred and ten cars invited to compete in the Indy 500. Out of those cars, only thirty-three are allowed to run the race. The final cars are chosen on the basis of time. During qualifying runs held on the first two weekends in May, each car goes out for a four-lap run. It goes as fast as it can four times around the two and a half mile track. The average speed of that four-lap run is the car's qualifying time. The thirty-three cars with the fastest qualifying times are the ones that line up to race the Sunday before Memorial Day. It is the car that qualifies, not the driver. Therefore, a team can change drivers before the race, if necessary.

Ray Harroun won the Indy 500 in 1911.

THE DEVELOPMENT OF THE CHAMP RACE CAR

The first American race cars were sports cars off the street. Racers chose the fastest cars they could find. Then they removed all the unnecessary parts to make them lighter and faster. But the cars still weighed between 2,000 and 2,500 pounds (907-1134 kg). That's 650 to 1,150 pounds (295-522 kg) more than today's race cars. These first race cars were two-seaters. The mechanic rode with the driver during the race to help fix any mechanical problems!

The first race cars were two-seaters.

Most of the engines were four and six-cylinder machines. They reached top speeds of between ninety and one hundred mph.

It took the French and Germans to show Americans how to make special race cars. The French Peugeot that won the 1913 Indy 500, for example, was far more advanced than the American cars. It had a superior engine that could have reached a top speed of 115 mph. Driver Jules Goux never had to use his top speed to win, because his car was so much faster than the others.

Both American and foreign cars, from 1911 to 1919, had serious oil leakage problems. Over one hundred four gallons — not quarts — of oil were lost by all the cars during one race! After one hundred miles, the bricks were slick with oil and there were many serious crashes.

In those early days of champ car racing, the time lost changing tires was a big problem. It took around sixty seconds for a pit crew to change a tire. (Today, it takes nine to eleven seconds.) Tire failures and blowouts were common. Most cars used at least eight or ten tires in a five hundred mile race. It bothered the drivers to waste so much time changing tires.

In 1914, there was a breakthrough. Knock-off hub nuts for the wheels were introduced. The nuts had pieces of metal that stuck out. They could be struck once with a hammer and would spin all the way off.

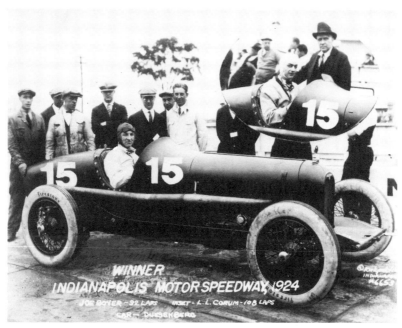

Joe Boyer won the 1924 Indy in one of the sleek, new cars.

Tires could now be changed in twenty to thirty seconds. Because of this, racers' times improved.

The champ cars built and raced during the 1920's, were faster for several reasons. Smaller, more advanced engines increased the speed and horsepower. Mechanics no longer rode with the drivers, which meant less weight. And in 1925, Firestone introduced the first racing tire. Up until that time, high-speed tires for sports cars were used. The "Balloon," as the first racing tire was called, was fatter and wider than any other tire. The Balloon put more

13

square inches of rubber on the track, improving the car's ability to take bumps and to stay on the track. Practically all the cars used the new Firestone tires in the 1925 Indy race. Qualifying speeds were up two to three mph. In fact, Pete DePaolo set a new track record of 101.13 mph. It was the first time the race was run at an average speed of over one hundred mph.

By the end of the 1920's, many of the champ cars cost as much as $15,000 to make. That was a lot of money at that time. Only a few wealthy owners could afford to build a car that cost so much. So, in 1930, the Contest Board of the American Automobile Association made a new set of rules. They hoped that the new rules would lower the cost of building a race car. The Board said cars now had to weigh at least 1,750 pounds (794 kg). Most of the cars that raced in 1929, weighed two to three hundred pounds (91-136 kg) less than that.

Increasing the minimum weight of the cars meant that builders could use more passenger-car pieces to make their cars. Those pieces weighed more, but cost less. The Contest Board also required that all champ cars again be two-seaters like passenger cars. That rule helped cut down the price of building race cars because builders could now use passenger car frames.

One piece of hardware to come out of this period in champ car racing was the Offenhauser race engine. The Offy, as it was called, was a simple, inexpensive engine that could be bought for less than $2,000. It could deliver one hundred fifty to two hundred horsepower. The Offy ran on gas/benzol fuel and required little care. It was a small, compact engine of around four hundred pounds (181 kg). By 1934, there were eleven of the new Offy engines in cars entered at Indy.

In 1936, the champ car was larger and heavier. Once again, the cars were two-seaters.

These larger, heavier cars, using inexpensive parts like the Offy engine, cut costs. But the number of serious crashes also increased. There was a series of fatal crashes in the early 1930's. As a result, more new rules were put into effect. Each car was limited to six gallons of oil for a five hundred mile race. It was hoped this would mean less oil spilled on the track and fewer accidents. Also, fuel-tank capacity was limited to fifteen gallons instead of the usual forty gallons. The race officials felt this would force more pit stops. More pit stops, they thought, would mean more tire changes and fewer blowouts. The new safety rules didn't work. The 1933 Indy 500 was the bloodiest in history. Five men were killed.

In 1936, officials got together and found ways to reduce the terrible accidents. The four turns on the speedway in Indianapolis were rebuilt. A ten-foot concrete strip was added around the outside of each turn. A broad, oiled-dirt apron was added on the inside of the turn, in place of the gutter. The outer wall was redesigned too, and slanted steeply inward. That pushed spinning cars back onto the track. The new turns were very effective. Two cars hit the new wall solidly during practice. Neither one left the track. There were no serious injuries. Officials had learned that there's no easy way to slow down a racer. The track just had to be made safer.

After the number of serious crashes decreased, race officials decided to loosen up the rules a little.

They wanted to give designers and builders more of a chance to develop new and better cars. It was time for some new ideas. For 1937, the American Automobile Association officials kept the same general rules that had been in effect since 1930. But they allowed superchargers on four-cycle engines. Superchargers were devices that forced more air into the carburetor to mix with the fuel and increase horsepower. Everyone had to run straight gasoline fuel. It was hoped that superchargers would make the cars go faster, but that gasoline would prevent the cars from going a great deal faster.

Then in 1938, American Championship racing changed over completely to International Grand Prix rules. These rules were the same rules used for all European Grand Prix races. The rules allowed, among other things, a free choice of fuel and single-seat cars. Racing officials thought the rule changes would encourage foreign manufacturers to send cars to race in the United States. They also hoped that some American racers would buy used Grand Prix team cars and run them in races. The officials were right.

Over the next few years more improvements were made on the Indy track. The four turns were paved with rock asphalt. The approaches to the turns were also paved. In 1940, the entire backstretch, the straightaway across from where the pits are located and the race starts and finishes, was also paved.

Lap speeds were faster because of the smoother track surface. The cars now reached average speeds of 128-130 mph. All in all, the new paving helped speed and safety. There were still some fatal accidents, but it was nothing like the record of the early 1930's.

When auto racing resumed after World War II, there wasn't much in the way of new cars. Racers and designers had been involved in the war. Most of the cars racing in 1946, had been raced before. It didn't take long, though, for championship racing to make a fast comeback.

The cars that made racing history after the war

George Robson won the first race after WWII.

were the "Blue Crown" Specials. These cars were very light, weighing only 1,650 pounds (748 kg). They used airplane gasoline. This gas was the key to their success. Cars could now get better mileage using less fuel. Drivers only had to make one pit stop for gas during the whole five-hundred-mile race.

In 1953, Championship racing entered the age of the roadster. The cars were called roadsters because they looked more like passenger cars than the race cars before them. In older race cars, the driver's body could be seen from the waist up. In the roadster, only the driver's head and shoulders were visible. The driver sat lower to the ground in the

Mauri Rose won the 1947 Indy in a "Blue Crown" special.

The Roadster dominated champ car racing between 1953-1963.

roadster, and the whole car was several inches lower than other race cars. The way the roadster was built put more weight on the left tires than on the right tires. This extra weight on the left, inside tires meant that in the turns, when the outside tires normally get an additional load, the weight on all four tires was more balanced. Roadsters were able to go around corners faster because of the better balance.

Roadsters dominated champ car racing for ten years. In that time, top lap speeds went from 138 mph to 150.73 mph. Everything was looking good for the roadster. But that, too, would change.

The racing world discovered that race cars could get around corners even faster if engines were placed toward the rear of the car instead of in the front. By 1965, there were only four front-engine roadsters entered in the Indy 500. The remaining twenty-nine cars all had rear engines. Also in 1965, the year after a fiery crash that killed two drivers, new rules changed champ car racing once more.

Because of the fires caused by the crashes, race officials encouraged the use of alcohol as fuel instead of gasoline. Alcohol doesn't catch on fire as easily as gasoline. Race officials also limited fuel-tank capacity to seventy-five gallons. They said that drivers had

Jim Clark won the 1965 Indy in one of the new rear-engine cars.

to make at least two pit stops, and that fuel hoses had to be hooked up whether fuel was transferred or not. To keep fuel from spilling in a crash, in-car fuel systems were changed. They were made crash-proof.

There is no question that the new rules changed champ car racing. Cars stopped getting smaller and lighter. Gasoline-based fuels disappeared overnight. More attention was paid to pit equipment like hoses and nozzles.

The new rules didn't succeed, though, in slowing the heavier champ cars down. They kept getting faster and faster during the 1970's. How? For one thing, car designers were able to increase engine power with turbocharging. Turbocharging involves taking gas from the exhaust of the engine. The gas is used to spin a small propeller inside the turbocharger. The propeller, in turn, sucks air in from outside and pushes it into the engine. This gives the engine more power and helps the car go faster.

Another new way of making cars go faster was to use ground effect. Simply put, ground effect is like flying upside down. Wings that look a bit like upside down airplane wings are attached to the bottom of both sides of the car. These side wings are called tunnels. Wind is sucked into the tunnels, pushing the car to the ground, giving it better traction and helping it go faster around turns. Cornering speeds rose dramatically in 1972. Bobby Unser was clocked at an astonishing 183 mph through turn-one at Indianapolis when he set a new lap record of 196.68 mph.

New champ car rules put a limit on ground effect. This is an attempt to slow cars down around corners and keep the cars as safe as possible. But as the history of champ cars shows, designers and engineers continue to find new ways to make cars faster, even when rules are adapted to slow cars down. Now we may see an improvement in engine horsepower or better racing tires. One thing is for sure — champ cars won't be slowed down for long, if at all.

Gordon Johncock, the 1973 winner, had a car with a turbo charged engine that used ground effect to increase speed on turns.

WHO BUILDS CHAMPION-SHIP RACE CARS?

Championship race cars are built mainly in the United States and in Europe. An English company called March builds more champ cars than any other single manufacturer. However, they don't race the cars they make. March builds cars and then sells them to racers. Racing teams, like Patrick in Indiana and Penske in Pennsylvania, not only build cars, but also race them in the champ car circuit.

Champ cars have gotten faster and faster over the years. They've also become more and more expensive to build. Remember how a lot of racing people were concerned about the high costs of building a race car way back in 1930? The fact has not changed. A new champ car today costs around $150,000 to build. That's without the engine which costs an additional $50,000!

There's no doubt that racing continues to be an expensive venture. That's why racing teams depend upon the sponsorship of racing-product companies like STP, Valvoline, Konis, and Bosch. These companies, and many others, pay to have their products advertised on race cars. Racing teams try to get enough money from these sponsors to pay for all their yearly expenses. Without this arrangement, most racing teams would be unable to afford the high cost of building and maintaining champ cars.

A racing team gets a car ready for a race.

HOW CHAMP CARS ARE BUILT

New ideas for race cars usually come from race car designers. These are often people with degrees in mechanical engineering. They use their creative and technical abilities to think of new ways of building race cars. Their challenge is to build cars that meet all the rules and regulations of the racing associations and still go fast enough to win races.

It takes two mechanical engineers working for

A mechanical engineer is drawing blueprints.

Patrick Racing Team a year and a half to design an all-new Wildcat. For their 1983 cars they decided not to rework the '82 model, but to create a totally new race car.

Rough drawings called layouts were made first. After making sure that every part of the car fit together perfectly, carefully designed plans, called blueprints, were drawn. Blueprints of a race car usually begin with the inside of the car, called the tub. The tub is the area in which the driver sits and the fuel cell (the container that holds the fuel) is located. The tub is built out of aluminum. All of the other parts of the car are fastened to the aluminum tub.

Once the blueprint of the tub is completed, the detailed blueprints for all other parts are drawn. These drawings include the wheels, transmission, and wings (for ground effect). Name a part, and there's a blueprint for it. The last blueprint drawn is of the exterior of the car. The blueprints for one champ car fill up an entire file cabinet with four drawers. That's a lot of work for just one car.

After the designers complete the blueprints, the manager and department heads of the racing team go over the plans very carefully. They need to know

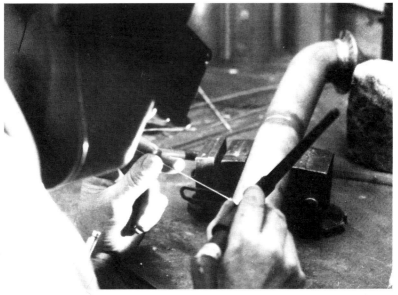

A mechanic is welding a header pipe in the machine shop.

A mechanic is putting valve seats in a cylinder.

which parts they have to make, and which parts and material can be ordered ready to use. Then the Machine Shop can get to work making the parts that have to be built.

THE MACHINE SHOP

The first thing the people in the Machine Shop do is design and make the tooling that is needed. Tooling is the machinery that is used to make the parts. After the tooling is made, the machinists can produce the parts. The machinists are responsible for making just about everything that is attached to the

The aluminum tub is resting on a jig.

tub, except the engine. It's hard work that keeps several people busy six days a week.

THE FABRICATION DEPARTMENT

The tub itself is built in the Fabrication Department on a special stand called a jig. The jig is perfectly level so that all the parts on the race car will line up correctly. The tub is the core of the race car and is made up of several different aluminum pieces that are fastened together. Patterns for the tub pieces are made first out of a heavy aluminum. Then a lighter aluminum is used to make the actual pieces from the patterns.

In order to make sure that all these pieces fit correctly before fastening them together permanently, little fasteners called clecoes are used. Clecoes can be fastened and unfastened easily. If a piece of the tub is the wrong size or shape, the clecoes are unfastened, and the piece is removed and fixed. Then the builder uses clecoes again to refasten the pieces.

Once the builder is sure all the tub pieces fit together, the entire tub is unclecoed, then riveted together. Riveting is a way of fastening metal together. Holes are drilled in two or more parts that need to be attached. Then what looks like an aluminum top hat is run through the holes. While a mechanic flattens the small end of the top hat with an air hammer, another worker holds it in place. This process is repeated until all the pieces of the tub are fastened securely. The finished tub weighs only eighty-five pounds (39 kg).

THE TRANSMISSION DEPARTMENT

The transmission for a car is made up of gears. These gears send power from the engine to the rear wheels. Race car transmissions have five gears, or speeds. But unlike passenger cars, there is no reverse gear. That means that a race car has to be pushed in order to go backward. This may surprise you, but there's a good reason for it. If a gear were to accidentally slip into reverse when the cars are going over two hundred mph, there would be a chance of a serious accident.

The molds or forms for the transmission case that holds the gears are usually made outside of the race-car shop. The transmission case, or box, is made out of magnesium. This is an even lighter weight metal than the aluminum used for the tub. The gears inside the transmission case are made out of steel. To make

A mechanic works on the transmission case.

the transmission case, a wooden mold that is the opposite, or mirror image, of the actual case is built. Next, sand is poured into the wooden mold. The sand used in casting the transmission mold is a special sand that has resin in it. Thus, the sand becomes firm and doesn't collapse when the wooden pieces are removed.

When the wooden pieces are pulled out, a void, or empty space, is left. That space is the area where the hot, melted magnesium is poured. It is left to harden and cool in the shape of the transmission case. After the magnesium is cool, the case is heat treated. The process of heat treating makes the case stronger. This process involves heating the case, cooling it, and heating it again at a lower temperature. Then the transmission case is cooled one final time.

Once the case has been heat treated, it is sent to a shop where all the machine work is done. Rough edges on the case are now smoothed, and holes for screws, called studs, are drilled.

All this work is completed in the Transmission Department.

Manufacturers that make the gears to go inside the transmission case start with a large bar of steel. That bar is made into what are called gear blanks, or pieces of material cut to specific measurements. The gear blanks are then put on a machine that cuts the gear teeth. It is the teeth on the gears that run together, or mesh, and force the gears to move.

THE ENGINE ROOM

Champ car race teams do not make their own engines. In fact, all champ cars today run on either the Cosworth engine or the Chevrolet stock-block engine. However, most race teams have their own Engine Room or Engine Department. Here, the engines are taken apart, tested, and then put back together again. Patrick Racing Team, for example, buys eleven engines for their three cars. These eleven engines are tested, and the best three are reserved for races. The others can be used if there are any problems with any of the top three engines.

Mechanics are putting an engine together in the engine room.

An engine installed in a champ car.

The engines are tested on a machine called a dynamometer. The machine actually simulates an engine running in a race car. By placing an engine on the dynamometer, mechanics can see how it works. The mechanic sits in a control room and "drives" the engine. By turning dials and pushing a throttle, information about engine pressure, air flow, fuel flow, and horsepower can be gathered. The driver can even figure out the mileage a particular engine will probably get. The dynamometer is an important testing tool. It provides valuable information. It also allows engines to be tested in the shop before being tested in a car.

BODY WORK

While the four departments — Machine, Fabrication, Transmission, and Engine — coordinate the making of the inside of the race cars, the body work that goes on the outside is being made. This work is often done by another company that has all the right tools and materials.

In order to make a mold for the body of a race car,

The dynamometer is used to test the engine.

A mechanic is bolting side panels onto the tub.

a solid, life-size clay model of the car is made first. Often these clay models are made by people who work for passenger car manufacturers. It's a time-consuming job that can take several months. Every inch of the car must be exactly as the designers drew it on the blueprints. In fact, designers often work with the people making the clay model. They mold the clay until it is an exact reproduction of the race car design.

Once the car designer is satisfied with the model, it is polished. Then a mold is made out of fiberglass. This mold becomes the permanent pattern from which the race car's outer body is made.

For the last several years, the outer body has been made out of a special material called carbon Kevlar composite. It is stronger than steel but very light. Fiberglass was used in the past, but Kevlar is stiffer, stronger, and lighter.

THE DRIVER'S SEAT

The outer body parts of a race car are not the only parts made from a mold. The driver's seat is molded, too. Every champ car driver has a seat especially made. The driver sits on a plastic bag, into which a two-part foam liquid is poured. The warm liquid hardens around the curves of the driver's body in five minutes. This forms the mold from which the actual fiberglass or Kevlar seat is made. A driver's seat that doesn't allow any movement is an additional safety feature of a champ car. The seat must also be comfortable. A driver in a five-hundred-mile race must sit for over three hours, often in extreme temperatures.

Race car drivers wear three safety belts: a shoulder belt, lap belt, and crotch belt. These three belt systems are hooked together with one latch that locks and releases all three at the same time.

THE CHASSIS DEPARTMENT

The car is put together in the Chassis Department. The mechanics usually start with the front suspension system — the parts that connect the tub to the two front wheels. Next they bolt the side panels to the tub. The fasteners they use are turned with a screwdriver. This makes it very easy to attach and detach the body work. The engine is then bolted to the tub, followed by the transmission. After that, the rear suspension system and the rear wing are attached. The rear wing is part of the ground effect system, just like the upside down wings under both sides of the car.

38

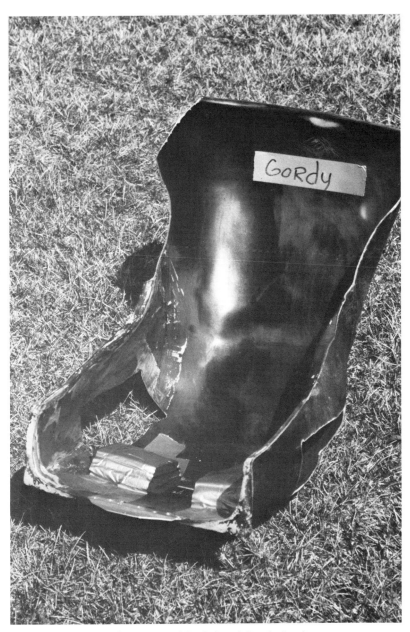

The seat is made from a mold of the driver's body.

Once the rear wing is in place, the wheels are installed. Finally, the nose (the front of the car) and the driver cowl (the piece that goes on top of the car with an opening for the driver) are bolted on. The race car is now complete and ready to be tested.

TESTING

Race cars are tested as much as possible before the racing season begins. Most of the testing is done during the winter months on tracks in Phoenix, Arizona and Atlanta, Georgia. That's a long drive from Indianapolis where Patrick Racing Team makes its cars. So, the cars are loaded on a large truck that is really a race car shop on wheels. The truck has a custom-built lift gate on the rear end that lifts a car to either the bottom or top level of the trailer where it is stored.

Normally, the truck hauls three race cars, two or three extra engines, transmissions and sixty wheels. The truck comes equipped with a welder that can weld any broken metal car pieces together, and a drill press that can drill holes. The truck also hauls all the pit equipment, including hoses and fuel tanks.

Testing is very expensive. A three-day test in Phoenix, for example, could cost Patrick Racing

A forty-foot "semi" is used to transport race cars and equipment to tests and races.

Team as much as $30,000 by the time all the costs are added up. A racing team must rent the race track on a daily basis. The track, in turn, supplies firemen, medical support, and people to clean the track. Often, one race team invites another team to share the cost of renting the track. But only one car is allowed on the track at a time.

Most of the testing of race cars, in the 1980's, centers around testing how well the ground effect is working. Mechanics test the tunnels at different levels and measure the air pressure going through. They also test things like suspension and tires. Drivers don't try to get the car up to fast speeds, however, until all the initial testing is completed. Then they can see how fast their cars can really go.

TAKING CARS APART

When testing is finished and the cars are returned to the Indianapolis shop, they are completely taken apart. In fact, the car is practically stripped down to the tub. A special machine called the magnaflux uses a dye that penetrates metal. This dye allows the mechanic to see any cracks in parts such as the engine, that otherwise couldn't be seen with the naked eye.

It takes two men almost a day to completely strip a car. To go through all the parts, and then put the car back together, usually takes three more days. The time is worth it. After checking all the parts, mechanics know they are sending a safe car back on to the track.

IT'S THE RIGHT CAR AND DRIVER THAT WIN

There have been many books and articles written about race car drivers. And there has been just as

The cars are off and running.

Gordon Johncock in the winner's circle after winning the 1982 Indy race.

much written about the excitement of the Indy 500 and other dramatic races. The driver or the race itself has always been the big story.

People who have driven for years would be the first to admit that they never could have won without a good car. Not one of these drivers would ever say that they could win with a poor car. Drivers know that it's the combination of the right car and the right driver that wins.

BLUEPRINT - A carefully designed plan of a car part.

CARBON KEVLAR COMPOSITE - A special woven fabric that is stronger than steel but very light and used for the body of a race car.

CLECOE - A temporary little fastener that allows the tub of a race car to be fastened and unfastened while it's being built.

DRIVER COWL - Piece of a race car that goes on top of the car with an opening for the driver.

DYNAMOMETER - Machine that simulates an engine running in a race car; used for testing engines.

JIG - A perfectly level stand on which the tub of a race car is built.

LAYOUT - A rough drawing.

MAGNAFLUX - A machine that uses a dye with a special light to penetrate materials; allows a mechanic to see cracks in car parts that otherwise could not be seen.

NOSE - The front of a race car.

PITS - Area off an entrance to race track where tires are changed, fuel is pumped, and any mechanical problems are worked on.

POLE SITTER - Car with the fastest qualifying time lines up for a race on the inside of the track in the first row.

RIVETING - A process used to permanently fasten the tub pieces together.

ROADSTER - Champ car that dominated racing from 1953-1963; called a roadster because it looked like a passenger car with only the driver's head and shoulders showing.

TRANSMISSION - Part of a car that transmits power from the engine to the rear wheels (or front wheels in a front-wheel-drive car).

TUB - The core of a race car, where the driver sits; all the other parts of a race car are attached to the tub.

TURBOCHARGING - Way of increasing engine power by taking gas from the exhaust of the engine and using it to spin a little propeller that sucks in air and rams it into the engine.

READ & ENJOY
EACH BOOK
IN THE SERIES!

TECHNOLOGY
HOW THINGS ARE MADE

BALLS
VIDEO GAMES
MICROCOMPUTERS
CHAMP CARS
BOOKS
CASSETTES & RECORDS
SHOES FOR SPORT
BIG RIGS